To.
....

....

With Love,
....

....

On
....

....

Copyright © 2019 by Sandie Darnell and Ashley Marie Kim
All rights reserved. This book or any portion thereof
may not be reproduced or used in any manner whatsoever
without the express written permission of the publisher
except for the use of brief quotations in a book review.

Printed in the United States of America

First Printing 2019

Original Poem by Ashley Marie Kim
Contact to sandiedd@mchsi.com
Contributor: Javen Campbell
Book Design and Art by Katie Joh
Contact to kt.johart@gmail.com
Instagram @kt.joh

ISBN 978-0-578-51778-0 (Hardcover)
ISBN 978-0-578-51918-0 (eBook)

An Angel's Gotta Do What An Angel's Gotta Do

by Ashley Marie Kim

Illustrated by Katie Joh

Angels can fly high

or low,

If you're in your mother's arms

or in your daddy's lap

or maybe you feel like
taking a quick quiet little nap.

If you're scared in your bed

or doing something
that you really dread...

They'll wipe

your tears

and fight against all your fears.

cause an angel's gotta do

what an angel's gotta do.

About this book

On the very day Ashley wrote an "Angel's Gotta Do" her mother received a call from Ashley's doctor confirming that she had a serious health issue. While her mother was praying for peace, comfort, and healing, her little girl, unaware of her own health condition, was being ministered to by God's angels through this poem. A short time later, Ashley returned to the hospital to receive the good news that she had been healed and no longer had the previously diagnosed condition. The poem was a reminder to her mother as we hope it is to you of Hebrews 1:1-14 and how God sends his angels as servants to care for us.

Bible verses

Psalm 91:11
"For he shall give his angels charge over thee, to keep thee in all thy ways."

Jeremiah 29:11
"For I know the plans I have for you, declares the LORD, plans to prosper you and not to harm you, plans to give you hope and a future."

Hebrews 1:1-14

www.ingramcontent.com/pod-product-compliance
Lightning Source LLC
Chambersburg PA
CBHW041352290426
44108CB00001B/23